A walk down Memory Lane

By Maura Renehan

God Bless

Maura Renehan 2015

ISBN: 978-1-909154-87-2

This book was published in cooperation with
Choice Publishing, Drogheda, Co. Louth,
Republic of Ireland.

www.choicepublishing.ie

Dedication

I would like to dedicate this book to my husband Ollie and my daughters Annmarie & Olive, their husbands Sean & Shane and my grandchildren, Bethany, Aoibheann, and Taylor.

Who have shared the rough and good times with me.

"The Joy of a dream come true"

I cannot do what you can do

You cannot do what I can do

But together we can do something beautiful for God.

Journey Through Life
Written By Maura Renehan
Co-written by Mary Prendergast

Surrounded by friends I pass all my days.
The sun as its shining I enjoy all its rays.
My body is weak buy my faith is strong.
With god on my side, we'll all get along.

As I journey thorugh life I carry a heavy load.
The road that I may follow will be my abode.
So don't be afraid you're of one of the chosen few.
Just hold his hand sincerely and he will guide you.

Chorus:

Be kind to everyone and love one another.
Treat everybody as sister and brother.
When your work on earth is done, it will seem so long.
He will take you home you'll never be alone.

So to yourself be true and your gifts you will renew.
For life has many seasons that pass along your way.
The shadow by your side will bring a brand new tide.
So hold on and remember, his arms are open wide.

Chapters

The Touch of the Master's Hand

'Twas battered and scarred, and the auctioneer
Thought it scarcely worth his while
To waste much time on the old violin,
But held it up with a smile.
"What am I bidden, good folks," he cried,
"Who'll start the bidding for me?"
"A dollar, a dollar. Then two! Only two?
Two dollars, and who'll make it three?"

"Three dollars, once; three dollars, twice;
Going for three..." But no,
From the room, far back, a grey-haired man
Came forward and picked up the bow;
Then wiping the dust from the old violin,
And tightening the loosened strings,
He played a melody pure and sweet,
As a caroling angel sings.

The music ceased, and the auctioneer,
With a voice that was quiet and low,
Said: "What am I bid for the old violin?"
And he held it up with the bow.
"A thousand dollars, and who'll make it two?
Two thousand! And who'll make it three?
Three thousand, once; three thousand, twice,
And going and gone," said he.

The people cheered, but some of them cried,
"We do not quite understand.

What changed its worth?" Swift came the reply:
"The touch of the Master's hand."
And many a man with life out of tune,
And battered and scarred with sin,
Is auctioned cheap to the thoughtless crowd
Much like the old violin.

A "mess of pottage," a glass of wine,
A game — and he travels on.
He is "going" once, and "going" twice,
He's "going" and almost "gone."
But the Master comes, and the foolish crowd
Never can quite understand
The worth of a soul and the change that is wrought
By the touch of the Master's hand.

"A Walk down Memory Lane"

By Maura Renehan

The 10th December 1940 was the day I was born. I am told my birth caused great excitement in the little cottage in Kilmacow that was to be my home for the next 30 years. My family was made up of my Mam and dad and my brother Nicholas who was 6 years my senior. He didn't share the same enthusiasm at my entry into the family circle as my Mam and dad did. I am told he would have gladly given me to anyone who would take me. I am glad to say he changed his mind quickly and as we were growing up I could always count on his support. Thinking back it is easy to understand his reluctance to allow me into his space. You see a brother and sister had died at birth in the years between his and my birth, so home was his domain. I should mention here that at the time I was born Mam was also caring for 2 of my cousins, 2 boys, Tom and Seamus, because their mother had died on the birth of Seamus. She also cared for her niece Eily whose Mother died from an asthma attack at the age of 30. I don't remember my grandmother but it seems that my Mam looked after her for some years before she died. She had been confined to bed from bad arthritis. When she died at the age of 66 she was so disabled that her knees had to be broken in order for her to fit into the coffin. At this point of the journey it is good to stop for a moment and get a picture in your mind of the people who made up our family unit. So now come with me and explore the tender years.

The Tender Years

I can recall events since I was about four years of age. I remember one Christmas Nicholas and I were sleeping in the back bedroom. During the night I woke and saw Dad take a white bundle of what must have been sheets and towels from the drawer. I thought different however and I woke Nicholas saying get up quick Dad has taken a baby from the drawer. We were not allowed down to the room for a while and when we were eventually allowed in we were thrilled to be shown our new brother by Nurse Carroll better known as Mother Carroll. She travelled all over Kilmacow and beyond delivering babies and would let you know for all time that she had delivered you. What a kind woman she was and what miles she covered on her bicycle day and night in the course of her work. Paddy was born on the 18th of December 1944.

Paddy, 2nd into right, back row

I remember Christmas Santa came with a red doll for me and a box of sweets. Nicholas got a football and a gun. Eily, Seamus, and Tommy also got their gifts as they had out grown Santa at that time. Dad and Mam exchanged token gifts as well. We had a great Christmas D.G, and Dad finished off the day by going to the card games in the local Ancient Order of Hibernians hall that night. That card game was always looked forward to and there were great prizes to be one. How times have changed. The Ancient Order of Hibernians Hall is now gone and in its place is a supermarket. Of course the supermarket is badly needed as no one would have dreamt even 40 years ago the increase of population that would take place in Kilmacow due to houses and apartments being built. Everything comes at a price of course, no one would like to go back to the hard times people had in the past. But I think there was a close bond among neighbours that was so strong. They formed their own health board and social services. You will understand what I

My cousin Joyce & I, outside the A.O.H. hall

mean as I go further into the story.

What comes to mind now is that one year it was my Mams birthday and we all got her a small gift. Then along comes Eily with two pairs of silk stockings. Mam enquired as how she got the money for the stockings. Mam and Dad couldn't hide their laughter when she replied innocently, "don't worry I got them on Appro from Harney's". Harney's was the shop in the village that sold everything at that time. Because they knew my Mother well, they would give her some things to bring home, and Mam would pick what she wanted and pay for them and give back the rest. That was Appro. Like any home where there are children there was sure to be happy and hard times. Mam and Dad where great providers. They worked hard for us. I thank god for security I felt within the family. I can remember as far back as to when I was four years of age. Mam would let me go up with Nicholas everyday to get milk from O'Keeffe's farm for our own use. We paid for quart measure every day, but they always filled up a sweet gallon for us. There was a saying at that time "THE SALT OF THE EARTH" and I truly believe that the O'Keeffe family lived up to that saying. The O'Keeffe's where also known as the Keeffe's of Crawn. The family where made up of four brothers and one sister and I could honestly say that we spent as much time on their farm as we did at home.

Ballybricken was renowned for its monthly cattle fair that was held every month and was where the farmers travelled from near and far to do there wheeling and dealing. Nicholas used to travel to the fair with the O'Keeffe's to help them take the cattle and mind them when needed. During the summer months Nicholas used to help them when they were busy. This was a great help to Mam and dad as the money he earned during the summer would help go towards books and uniforms going back to school.

Ballybricken Fair

On Saturday evening the bus would drop off meat for the O'Keeffe's which had been bought in Waterford from a well known butcher by the name of O'Gorman. My Mam would bring it up to their house and we would take turns at twisting the fan at the side of the fire which would stir the fire into a faster flame. When we paid for the milk on a Saturday Katie would always give us a few pence back for ourselves which we were delighted with. There was another family who lived in Crawn known as John and Mary Moore. They were great people and were always there for you if needed. Another well known family who lived in Crawn would have been the Walsh family. Their son Michael still lives in Dangan to this day. There was a great bond between all of them and all of the immediate neighbours. The farmers that we have been speaking of used to have fields near our house.

My Mam, the 3rd person in the front, on the right

When they worked near us Mam would put a bit extra in the pot so that there would be enough to go around. This arrangement was greatly appreciated and they reciprocated by bringing us eggs, milk, country butter etc so everyone was happy.

When Paddy was very young he would look out to see the Moore's coming home from Waterford on a Saturday evening. As they passed along in there pony and trap "THE ROLLS ROYCE" of that time they would throw out a bag of sweets onto the road which Paddy was only too glad to pick up. When Mam heard what was happening she was mortified and told him not to do it again. But John and Mary were disappointed and told my Mam not to stop him again.

Oh to have a little house....

O, to have a little house!
To own the hearth and stool and all!
The heaped up sods against the fire,
The pile of turf against the wall!
To have a clock with weights and chains
And pendulum swinging up and down!
A dresser filled with shining delph,
Speckled and white and blue and brown!
I could be busy all the day
Clearing and sweeping hearth and floor,
And fixing on their shelf again
My white and blue and speckled store!
I could be quiet there at night
Beside the fire and by myself,
Sure of a bed and loath to leave
The ticking clock and the shining delph!
Och! but I'm weary of mist and dark,
And roads where there's never a house nor
bush,
And tired I am of bog and road,
And the crying wind and the lonesome hush!
And I am praying to God on high,
And I am praying Him night and day,
For a little house – a house of my own
Out of the wind's and the rain's way.

Work and play

As I said before, I always felt secure at home. Maybe this feeling came from being able to have what I needed when I needed it and also being able to go on trips and days out. Looking back I can thank Mam and Dad for that. They both worked hard for us kids. Dad worked for Iarnrod Eireann. He cycled from Kilmacow as far as Thomastown, Newross and sometimes Clonmel. He also cycled to Enniscorthy. When he had to work there he needed to stay there for a week. We missed him a lot on those weeks he was away. Paddy and I used to wait for him on a Saturday in a little gap on the turn of the road. We would see him coming along and when he got closer to where we were waiting, we would run to meet him. You could see the delight on his face when he saw us. He would walk up the road with us to our house and we would tell him all our news of the week. Twas his practice to make sure we had fire wood for the week, and he would also check to make sure that the vegetable garden was in order. He brought the orders he used to get for his veg from the man in greengrocer shops in Ballybricken. This was the pattern of our life for a few months every year. Then when that work was finished Dad would return to Waterford train station and a normal way of life resumed.

Left to Right: Maura & Ollie, Maura's Dad, Nicholas Rowe and Aunt Maggie Kirby

Even though the road where I lived was very quite there was only our house and the forge on the road, yet because of all the farmers coming and going from the forge the place was never lonely.

The Forge Road, Narabane, Kilmacow

A little memory I have from these times also was Mam bringing us to Waterford on the Suir Valley Bus on a Saturday morning. She would bring us in turns. Our first call would be to Woolworths, it was like Aladdin's cave to us. It held everything to draw a child's attention, from sweets to small toys, books and school stationary. She used to tell us to keep our hands off of everything, it was like her mantra. The counter display was so low that she was afraid that we would take or break anything. As we walked around the shop we would be looking for different items such as toys and sweets. She usually softened and bought us some little treat. Ice-cream was always welcome in the summer time and when Mam was finished doing her shopping and talking to friends that she would meet on her way, she would then bring us to the ice-cream parlour and buy us all an ice-cream. My favourite was a Knickerbocker Glory that was served in a long tall glass with a wafer biscuit and strawberry syrup. I love and cherish those days that I spent with my Mam as a child. When we were finished we would head back for the bus and make our way home tired but happy after our outing. Another day that we looked forward to was our annual trip to Tramore Beach. This day was made possible by my uncle Nick and Aunt Alice. Uncle Nick would get up early on that morning Aunt Alice and Mam would also be up very early that morning preparing a feast for us to have on the beach. We also brought our buckets and spades ready for any fun that was available to us. I must mention here that Uncle Nick's daughter Mary would also come with us. She was an only child but wasn't spoiled, and she was full of fun and would be equally at ease playing with boys or girls. She was interested in music and played the button accordion from the age of 3. She is still involved teaching set dancing and still plays the accordion. It happens that she is the only cousin on my Mams side still living around Kilmacow today so I value her friendship very much. In any event getting back to our trip to Tramore, Uncle Nick would arrive at our gate accompanied by Aunt Alice and Mary. They were travelling in the Rolls Royce of the day which was a pony and trap. Mam Paddy and I joined them in the trap and off we headed for Waterford Railway Station. Uncle Nick helped us go into the station and then headed back home promising to collect us at 6pm.

There was great banter and plenty of noise on the train going down and we children where really excited. When we got to Tramore Mam and Aunt Alice would take the picnic basket from the train and under there watchful eyes we would make our way to the beach. We weren't long changing into our bathing costumes and after being blessed with holy water by the grownups we ran into the water splashing and jumping round and round. It was great fun. Our Mams at this time were feeling hungry so we dried ourselves and got dressed. They opened the basket and one of them brought a large tea pot over to a woman who was providing boiling water at a minimal cost. There was lovely little snacks crisps, sweets, cocktail sausages and a variety of drinks for us. She set it all out on a lovely picnic blanket and it looked beautiful. We ate heartily and with the help of some children whom we had befriended we soon left back clean plates. After that we went for a ride on a pony which was led up and down the beach by a man. This would be his business during the summer months. We really enjoyed that. When we were finished we would head for the amusement park and spent some time there on the rides such as swinging boats, chair planes and our favourite the bumpers. The ghost train was good for anyone who would venture on it. Soon it was time for us to head back to the train station and head on our merry way home. Uncle Nick was there waiting to bring us home. We were tired but happy and look forward to another year.

Early School Days

Life never stays the same. When I was four years of age plans where put in place for me to start school.

I started in the Presentation Convent School in Kilmacow September 1945. Mother De Lourdes was my first teacher. My cousin Eily was still going to that school at the time, so she brought me down to school on my very first day.

I was allowed sit with Eily in her class that day, which brought me some kind of comfort for such a big change in my life.

The second day the nun asked me to go to my own class. She brought me up to a wooden building where I recognised Phyllis and Joan Cooke whom I was used to playing with in the field between our houses. This softened the ordeal somewhat. Maureen Dowling was a neighbour who also played with us, so it didn't take long for me to settle in.

The Presentation sisters were the ones who looked after our educational needs at the time. They were strict, some were cross and there where one or two who were very kind. But I think all in all, they gave us a well grounded solid education for life.

School Picture taken outside of Mooncoin hall
on the day of the Gregorian chant, Maura 2nd row from right

Mother De Lourdes was the one who taught me for the first three years. She was very patient but she wasn't fooled easily. One weekend when I was in first class I had some maths to do as homework. I didn't have a problem with maths. It was probably my best subject. That weekend some friends called to my house, so I decided to give maths a miss. When I got to school on the Monday I asked the girl who sat next to me to let me have the answers to the homework I hadn't done. She gave it to me without hesitation. The nun came in went up to the blackboard and proceeded to correct our maths. All was well until one maths problem came up to which everyone had a different answer. Down she comes to check our homework and when she looked at mine, I wished the ground would swallow me up. She didn't bat an eyelid. She enquired very calmly where my homework was I gave her the lame excuse that I left my copy at home. She very kindly decided to send a senior student to my house to get the said copy book. Needless to say a lot of questions had to be answered between school and home. That day I learned a life lesson thanks to Mother De Lourdes "honesty is the best policy". What a tangled web we weave when first we start out to deceive.

Looking back on the years spent in that school there was great discipline taught. We got every opportunity to learn if we had the urge to do so. Any of the girls who enrolled into secondary school were very welcome there as the nuns had them well focused and prepared for the years ahead.

Fun Times

On weekends Mam did her best to provide a special dinner for us all. Roast beef with all the trimmings and eve of pudding for dessert was always my favourite. When we were finished Mam would get a few old coats and soon we were ready to climb the Knock field opposite our house. Mam always brought socks to darn and the Sunday newspapers to read. She loved the view from the top of the hill. On a nice sunny day we had great fun pulling each other up and down the hill on the old coats that we had brought.

Our friends from across the way where also there and we girls had great fun playing rounder's and cabby house.

At this time Tommy Seamus and Nicholas where still at school and all three loved to play hurling in their spare time. Seamus was a loveable rogue; Mam often told the story how a lot of children had been out of school because they had the mumps. Tom was very sick and Mam kept him at home, Seamus came home that evening and showed all the signs and symptoms of mumps so Mam kept him home from school the next day. But as the day went on he was restored to good health as if a miracle had happened. Needless to say he was sent running to school the next morning. His teacher Mr Lynch asked him why he hadn't been in school the previous day. He answered "I was expecting the mumps sir".

The Days of Innocence and Love:

By now I was coming up to seven years of age. I was one of about 20 children who were to receive the First Holy Communion that year. The nuns where committed to giving us a good knowledge of God and his love for us. We also had a good training in the home. We generally knew our morning and night prayers before starting school. Of course the rosary was the key to heaven in Ireland at that time. Because Ireland had suffered so much persecution for their faith in the not so distant past, they trusted Our Blessed Mother to see them through their troubles and she didn't fail them. There is a mass bush about half a mile from Kilmacow village a legacy of the days when priest said mass at great risk to their safety. The people came from miles trusting in Our Lady to bring them safely to the celebration of the Eucharist and then to protect them as they made the long journey from their homes.

Mass Bush, half mile up the Creamery Hill in Kilmacow

When I was preparing for First Holy Communion it was the custom of all the children to go to the mass bush and put a little chip from the bark of the tree in there shoe to help them in all the exams and important events in their life. So the evening before my communion I went with some of my friends to the mass bush. The ground surrounding the mass bush was thronged but the bigger girls worked hard to give all of us younger ones a little piece of bark and so we all went home happy.

My first communion day was a very special day. The sun was shining and we were all very happy. Mam had washed us and got our clothes ready the night before. Eily, Tom, Seamus, Nicholas, and Paddy where dressed in their best Sunday clothes. But I felt like a million dollars. My hair was done in ringlets Mam had gone through great pains to have them looking perfect for the day. Dressed in my lovely white dress and veil my white shoes and stockings and my little bag containing my new white prayer book and white gloves I couldn't be happier.

When I arrived at the church I went to the front seat where all my classmates where assembled under the watchful eye of Anna Quinlan who stood in for the nuns. They were not let outside the convent gates in those days. I remember the mass was lovely. We all had some little part to do. The choir sang lovely hymns for the occasion. It is a day I will always remember. After mass our parents collected us from our seats. All of us children admired each other's clothes. Then Mothers and Fathers too proceeded to Harney's and Kathleen French's shop for ice-cream and sweets bought with the money given to us by neighbours relatives and friends. Then we came home and the day ended with a lovely meal which some of my cousins and friends shared with us. And so a day that was simple but happy came to a perfect end.

About this time too a change was about to take place in our family structure. Tom and Seamus where now coming to the time where they would leave national school Tom had done very well at national school and in fact he obtained a scholarship for his secondary education. Seamus was more into cooking which he was very good at and in his spare time he was involved in the local drama society under the direction of Pat Knox a local man who had a great interest in stage productions. Concerts where held in an old hall which is still standing today. It was a great facility for the young people who loved acting at that time. They travelled to Wexford and other places to put on a show. Those taking part enjoyed themselves as did the audience who where made up of young and old. Seamus used to sing the cod liver oil song and it was a comedy song and he has happy to give it his best. Anyway their father who had been working in England since the two boy's mother died had met a very nice young woman who he was instantly attracted to. They went out together for a few years then decided to get married I believe it was a lovely wedding ceremony. They went back to England after that but after a few months had passed they decided to come to Ireland and bring back the boys to England with them. It caused great upheaval at home at the time. Because Nicholas was nearer to age as the two cousins than he was to Paddy and myself. He missed them a lot. Mam encouraged the boys to have a little get-together with their friends before they departed. It was a great success. They talked and laughed recalling pranks they shared through the school years. I know dad used to be exasperated with Seamus when he tried to teach him the bible. One night dad asked him trying to bring lightness into the situation "where was Moses when the light went out" he answered "we didn't come to that part yet". They talked of the times when Seamus would go with bucket and rope to bring water from the well at the back of our house. You had to drop the bucket down with the rope, fill the bucket and pull it back up but Seamus thought it would be a better idea to drop the bucket down the well and bring back the rope. Needless to say Mam wasn't impressed but you can be sure he didn't get away scot free, there's more than one way to skin a cat.

However, none of this matters now that our cousins were going away from us. They left from Rosslare.It was my first personal experience of emigration and I didn't like it. I think Mam missed them more than any of us as she looked on them as her own. Life goes on and we had to get back to a routine. I remember it was the month of May. There was devotions every Sunday evening in our church. I think it was the same in all surrounding parishes. The hymns were lovely but what I really looked forward to on a nice sunny evening was Mam and Dad and Jack and Mrs. Dowling walked home by the river, a longer route I know, but what scenery. All of us children were free to run and play as we made our way home.

Music of Life

BY MARIAN HILL

I was at the Mass of Remembrance for the Waterford branch of The Irish Kidney Association.

One of the patients Marian Hill now deceased recited this poem with great feeling from the alter.

As she returned to her seat I congratulated her.

She handed me the poem which I dearly loved, and felt honoured to have it. Hence it has made an appearance in my first book.

Music of Life

Written by Marian Hill

On many a summers evening.

As the sun was going down.

Granddad would play his fiddle.

And I would act the clown.

So many songs I sing then.

My voice so sweet and clear.

It feels like only yesterday

The music I still hear.

I often asked my grandad,

What he thought my life would be,

The firelight flickered in his eyes

As he said these words to me.

Sing your songs and play your tune

But learn to listen too

Be kind and understanding

And to yourself be true

Take a little time each day

To find out who you are

Then rich or poor whatever comes

You'll always be a star.

First Time Away From Home

Clearly I remember where Eamon and Collette Rice live now there was a little shelter in the ditch in the shape of an arch and up to this day this spot is known as "GOD IN THE BOTTLE" A travelling man used to come at different times during the year and camp there. He had a rather unique gift. He was able to put a crucifix into

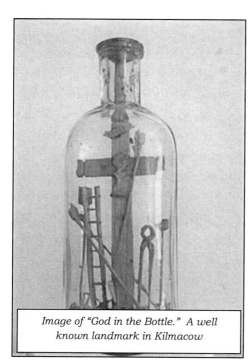

Image of "God in the Bottle." A well known landmark in Kilmacow

bottles and then cork them. He was the only man I ever saw with this gift. Years after I saw the same bottle with a crucifix in it at my husband's grandfathers home. It brought back great childhood memories.

In those days the doctors came to the school to give us general checkups. When I was about 8yrs old my throat was giving me a lot of pain and when the doctor saw my tonsils he immediately decided to send me to St Lukes Hospital Kilkenny with four other girls who were also going. We waited a few weeks and then one day we were notified that we would be going by ambulance that weekend. I was excited at first getting my case and everything ready. But when the ambulance stopped at our gate I could feel the first twinge of loneliness set in. I missed Mam very much as I had never spent a night away from her before. The ambulance man was very nice so we didn't mind the journey. A nurse met us at reception and admitted all five of us to the same ward. We were made to fast over night. The next morning I was one of the first to be brought to the operating theatre. The mask that they used to put me out was sickening I will never forget it. It took a day or more to get to my real self again.

There was what I would call a sergeant major of a nurse in Kilkenny at that time. One evening up she came to me with some concoction. I remember I couldn't swallow it and I made this known to the nurse but she wasn't having any of it and proceeded to put it down my throat. By now I was coming to understand that this nurse didn't understand English, so I helped her by leaving it on the floor. We had come to Kilkenny on Friday. On Sunday night the girls who were with me where told they would be going home next day. I was a bit upset because I had to stay back it seems I was still bleeding a bit. The doctors wanted everything to be right before I was discharged. I eventually went home the following Friday. The ambulance brought me home. But when I came to the top of the road I told them I only lived around the corner and he had plenty of room to turn at the place where we were. He helped me down from the ambulance and said goodbye and was gone. He wasn't to know that I lived slightly further away from the cross roads than I told him. You see I had a little plan in mind to call on blacksmith Tom to let him know I was home. I had a little chat with Tom before I went home.

Mam was delighted that I was back again but was a bit bewildered that the ambulance driver left me off before coming to my gate. However all's well that ends well. No harm had been done and we where soon back at school as normal.

About this time too, Eily who had been with us since she was 3 years old was getting itchy feet and looked at the papers everyday to see what jobs where out there for her. She eventually settled on an Irish doctor living in England who had a wife and two children who she would have to care for while he and his wife were at work. She went over in the month of May. We missed her as she had helped Mam a lot at home. They had a great mother daughter relationship. Mam felt happy when she opened a letter delivered by the postman. It was from Eily and she told us she was so happy with the family. They treated her as if she was one of their own. Mam just looked at the Sacred Heart picture on the wall and thanked god.

One by one the family seemed to be leaving the nest. But they knew the door was always open for them in Kilmacow. The months rolled by after that nothing seemed to upset the rhythm of our life for a while. But we never know what's around the corner. In October 1949 Eily let Mam know that she was coming home for 2 weeks holidays. Everyone was excited and it so happened that our annual religious exam was taking place on that day too. I had all new clothes ready for the occasion. Kitty Flavin R.I.P had knitted me a beautiful jumper and her Mam who was a dress maker had made me a beautiful pink pleated skirt. When I woke up that morning I told Mam that my neck was stiff. She thought I was pulling a fast one. It was obvious however after I attempted to stand on the floor and was unable to do so that something was wrong. Mam went to the post office and rang Doctor Breslin the Iarnroid Eireann doctor. He came out from Waterford as quickly as possible. He said that he would call again that evening. When he came to me in the evening Dad had just come in from work. The doctors told Dad that he thought I had polio. Mam and Dad where devastated to hear this. I saw my Dad cry unashamedly for the first time in my life. The ambulance came next morning and Dad came with me as far as Kilkenny. He went back to Waterford in an ambulance returning there. I was sad to see him go but the stretcher I was on was placed in another ambulance and we headed for Dublin. I was admitted to a ward with mostly older people and there was one girl about 15 years of age and she was the one who would share fun time with me in the future. The CMO of Kilkenny Health Services came to visit at home and informed Mam and Dad that they were not to go outside the gate. She said people could leave food and essentials outside the gate for them. But Doctor Breslin also came and told Mam and Dad that he had been to see me in Cork Street and had been told that there was no restriction on visiting in the hospital and polio was not contagious.

At this time I was nearly 100 % paralysed and I was only there a few days when Mam's aunt Bee came in to see me. She was in her eighties at the time. She brought me a lovely relic of blessed Martin. She told me that she had been to St Dominic's church in Dublin and that she had got a mass offered up for me by Father Coffey. She asked me to hold the relic all night in my hand and to say a prayer to Blessed Martin. I did this and next morning when I woke I just tried to see if I could move and to my surprise I was able to move my hand a little I was delighted. To this day I am convincened that it was through the intersession of Blessed Martin now best known as St Martin that I was cured. I would also give some credit to the head doctor and I can remember to this day the kindness of a young nurse from Wicklow called Nurse Moore who was ever so kind to me. I spent 3 months in the hospital and got up to a lot of mischief. That Christmas the ground was covered in snow but a girl of 15 whose name was Pauline brought me for a spin in a wheelchair all round the grounds of the hospital in the depths of the snow. We were nearly responsible for a few nurses having heart attacks. At the time I was in hospital I had a head of long blond curly hair. Pauline said to me "wouldn't you like to have short hair like me, you wouldn't be getting your head pulled off every morning when they are brushing it". So she very nicely asked a nurse for a loan of a scissors. We went into a toilet and she started to cut. She didn't use a ruler and my hair was cut into a zig zag pattern. The nurses again nearly lost it when they saw the state I was in. They dreaded what Mam and Dad would say when they came to see me. But Mam wasn't a bit put out. She said "what difference is it about the hair once I got better".

I didn't feel the 3 months going as I was very content in the hospital and Mam and Dad made arrangements that Dad would come one week and stay with aunt Bee and then when he went home Mam would come up and stay for another week and so it went on. On my ninth birthday which was spent in the hospital the nurses put on a birthday party for me and Billy Fennelly, who was a baker in Harney's and good friend of the family, made a big birthday cake which was enjoyed by all.

At Christmas we had a great time in the hospital. There was parties and carol services and Santa came with loads of gifts for everyone. In January 1950 I eventually was discharged from hospital and thank God I was able to go back to school that April and have lead a relatively good and happy life since.

I must mention Mrs Agnes Knox at this time. As she lived nearer to the school than we did she told Mam to let me come down every day for my lunch to her house. They had been friends for years and Mam was delighted with the offer. Every weekend Mam would leave in what was needed for my lunch for the week and Agnes did the rest. This continued until I left the national school. Agnes is now gone R.I.P but her kindness and what she did for me will never be forgotten.

A Man of the Roads

The family put the final touches to the preparations for the big feast day coming up the next day. There was a loud knock at the front door. My husband Jim answered. There was a lot of whispering in the hall which seemed to go on for a long time but really it was our anxious curiosity which made it seem so. As we were about to collapse with worry, we could hear the echo of many loud footsteps approach the living room. Looking in the direction of the door I nearly fell with shock to see my husband accompanied by a policeman and our next-door neighbour carrying and pulling a little frail old man. He was covered in blood and clay, I got a cushion and blanket and they put the poor man on the couch.

My daughter and I washed him as best we could and dressed his cuts. Thankfully he wasn't as badly injured as we first thought. While we had been cleaning the poor man, the policeman had been busy on the phone enquiring as to the identity of the stranger.

It turned out he was a man of the roads, but his people were from the locality. We gave him some tea and toast and he seemed a little brighter. After some discussion with the guard and my family we decided to leave him rest for the night on the couch.

Next morning we were all going to early mass. My eldest daughter and her friend offered to stay with our guest whom they had decided to call Noel. On our return from mass we were surprised to find the two girls and Noel busy preparing Christmas dinner. They seemed to have taken a shine to Noel. He seemed to be in great spirits and little worse for his ordeal the previous night, which seemed to be as a result of a little seasonal over indulgence. The girls then offered us drinks of various strengths which helped to warm and relax us. At this stage Noel was fitting in with everyone like an old sock.

Soon we made our way to the Christmas tree. There were presents exchanged and Noel hadn't been forgotten. At about three o'clock we sat down to dinner. Noel asked if we had an accordion. Sure enough my daughter had one in her room which she gave to him. The music that he brought from it was varied and beautiful and nothing short of the touch from the master's hand.

At the end of the day we all agreed that it was the best Christmas we ever had. Noel departed the next day as the call of the roads would always be in his blood. We will never forget him and I hope he will call if he passes this way again. It really taught our family that Christmas has nothing to do with big spending, but more about thinking and sharing with others. If you stretch out your hand in friendship you receive back a hundred fold.

A Change Of School

After my recovery from polio I went back to school. The nuns decided that because I had missed so much time it would be to my advantage to stay back a year. I had started school very young in the first place so I wasn't out of place with my new class mates.

In 1954 when I was in sixth class Sr. Assumpta prepared us for our primary cert examination. This was a government examination for which we got a certificate basically to prove that we were proficient in the 3 RS reading writing and arithmetic. We were all excited and anxious about it. Sr Assumpta gave us extra help after school each evening for some weeks before the exam.

When the weather was good we went down to the bank of the Black Water River which was at the back of the school to study. This brings back great memories of seeing the swans glide along gracefully. It was a beautiful scene. I don't know if they are still there now.

On the day of the exam, we were all encouraged to go to early mass. Anyone who lived near the church were asked to bring one of the girls who lived further away to breakfast in their house. I brought a girl home that lived about 2 miles from the school. We were in sight of our house when the front wheel tyre blew out and threw me from the bike. I wasn't badly hurt but my right arm was swollen and stiff. I was frustrated going back to school but Sr. Assumpta in her wisdom encouraged me to go ahead and sit the exam. She decorated my arm with medals and relics etc and to complete her caring she included a note for the examiner explaining the reason for the poor quality of my writing. Luckily I did pass the exam as did all my class mates.

Summer holidays were coming up at that stage. Nicholas worked in a garden centre in Waterford at that time. Paddy got work with a farmer from around the area. This kept him busy. In the evening he went to the hurling field with his friends. There was very little vandalism done in those days. Mam was very busy at the time as well. There was no electricity or no gadgets to make life easy. She had a set day for the regular jobs. This included cleaning the range, scrubbing floors, washing, ironing and cooking. There were no expensive cuts of meat but that didn't stop her serving up meals fit for a king. Needless to say I had to help Mam with the chores. I didn't always do them willingly but looking back I am glad she instilled a work ethic which has stood me well down the years.

Singing Competition

During those years there was a school singing competition named Gregorian Chant. The mass was sung in Latin on that day.

All the schools in the diocese took part. All the children looked forward to that time every year.

The occasion always merited a new uniform.

There was a trophy to be won every year.
Our school won it a few years and we loved having the day off from school and having fun meeting all the children from other schools.

A Time of War

Now that I have gone so far down memory lane I look back and feel that I am surely skipping over some events that were part of our childhood in Kilmacow.

So as we move forward together, I will try to bring those events to life.

I recall during my early school days, alot of my school mates brought their cousins from England to our school.

They enrolled and seem to stay a long time.

It was only in later years that we realised the children were brought back to Ireland by their Irish parents to keep them relatively safe from all the bombing in England during World War Two.

Favourite Old Memories

When people died in the area my Grandmother was always called on to help lay them out and get them ready for their journey to heaven.

One day when my Mother was very young my Gran was in the neighbour's house where a member of the family had just died. She asked Mam to go home and get the bed linen which was stored in a special drawer where it could be located when required.

My grandmother got worried when my mother didn't appear to be coming back. She looked out and saw Mam coming along "what kept you" Gran asked, Mam answered, "I was airing the sheets".

Something I did enjoy was helping to make jam for the winter. We picked gooseberries, blackcurrants, blackberries, and apples.

Mam bought lots of sugar. She would have saved jam jars and stored them away. Now when she took them out, and the kitchen would be full of a lovely aroma of delicious fruit boiling gently in a large saucepan. This continued until the liquid had thickened to the right consistency. Then she would let it cool for a while and lastly the jars were filled with this lovely jam. No bought jam could ever equal it. I also remember Mam filling a zinc bucket with water and putting in a substance called water glass.

Then she would put in eggs which were not needed for our daily use when the hens where laying well. This insured that she would have ample supply of egg for baking when winter came.

Mary and Nicholas Rowe - Maura's Grandparents

Confirmation

As well as sitting for my primary cert, I made my confirmation on the 8th of April 1954. Because confirmation took place every 3 years in my parish, the age under which you could not receive confirmation was 11 years old. I was only 10 years old the last time confirmation took place. So I was 13 years old and preparing for the sacrament which was to bestow all the gifts of the Holy Spirit and through this spirit to strengthen our faith.

Confirmation was a big event. We seemed to have many hours of religion taught to us for months beforehand. The bishop would ask some questions and we had to have the answers ready. For some reason we never heard of anyone failing that exam.

The year of my conformation April 1954, we were the first group to be confirmed in the newly renovated church. Bishop Collier was the one who confirmed us. He wasn't very well that year so Fr Mullin and another priest examined us on religion and so after that the bishop was left to confirm us.

The adults used to say that he would give us a slap on the jaw but that never materialised. He came across as a nice man and we all enjoyed the day. It's amazing how parents can rise to such occasions every child was turned out beautiful. I think that was the first confirmation that girls didn't have to wear a white dress and we were all pleased about that. Some of the taller girls where getting nylon stockings for the occasion and some were wearing white ankle socks. Mam was in favour of me wearing ankle socks. But I was anxious to have nylons like my friends. I kept coaxing Dad to get round her. Eventually Dad said "ok I will give you the money myself". I was delighted as that was the custom at that time. We were invited by the bishop to take the pledge promising to abstain from alcoholic drink until we reached 21 years of age.

When the ceremony was over we all came together outside the church. Photos were taken as lovely keepsakes like the they do at the present time. There was a very big crowd of parent's, aunt's, uncles and neighbours. Some of them were invited by Mam and Dad to come back home with us. We were thrilled to be able to play with them then we had something to eat. We played for a short time as it was getting late. People where anxious to say their goodbyes and make their way home. After the confirmation we were given a day off from school.

To my delight Mam and Dad made plans to bring Paddy and myself to Aunt Bea's house in Dublin. Dad had a family pass from Iarnrod Eireann, so it was easy to arrange.

I remember going to Aunt Beas house. She was thrilled to see us. Aunt Bea had a lot of sadness in her later years. But I will save that story for another time. While we were there we visited the National Museum. I was sad at the time to read the letter written by Kevin Barry to his Mother just before he was executed. I think it was because he was so young that I was so emotional. We also visited the Zoo in the phoenix park. We were thrilled to see all the animals and birds who originated in far off countries such as bear's, lion's, tigers, and monkeys etc. We went for a short ride on the elephant and we had a drive in the park on a pony and trap where we saw monkeys, giraffes, zebras and many others. It was well worth the visit. Before we left for home we went and enjoyed a nice picnic. We hated going away from the park but Moore St had to be seen before we left Dublin. Moore St., was amazing. All the stalls where cramped together but it was unbelievable. The traders had a mantra which went something like this "six pence a lb tomatoes and plums six pence a lb do you want some Mam". The traders were steeped in the old customs of Dublin. The stalls were a mass of colours of all the fruits of the season blending naturally together. One of the traders name was Rosie and she was looked up to as the Queen.

The Moore St traders gave value to their customers and the customers were loyal to them in return. We returned to Dublin many times after that but that one time will always hold a special place for me.

Transition Year

The summer after our confirmation I will remember fondly always. About five of us who had been in 6th class together got summer work with a fruit farmer Gerard Spencer of Sliver Spring Mooncoin. At that time there wasn't much employment in the Mooncoin area so Spencer's filled a very important role in the area and he was a lovely man to work for. He had men in the Dairy he had another group in the glass houses as well as many men doing general farm work.

The women who worked there were delighted to be able to bring their young children with them every day. The mums saw to it that they were employed picking fruit. Every Friday Mr Spencer paid us. Every man woman and child where paid the going rate.

One of the girls had an accordion Mr Spencer put boards down in the yard so we were able to enjoy ourselves dancing and singing during lunch hour.
One funny incident when we were picking apples one day. One young fellow was on a ladder singing "I just can't wait to be with my baby tonight", Mr Spencer comes up behind him and says "it would be a good idea to pick a few apples while you're waiting".

During that year in the summer Fr Mullin decided to run a Carnival also known as a fete. In order to help defray the cost of repairing the church which had being badly burnt a few months previously. There was a marquee there in which a top band played every night. I went with Mam and Dad and as I was only about 15 or so I wasn't considered old enough to go in. Nevertheless there was a lot to be enjoyed i.e. hurling matches, pony racing, pongo, wheel of fortune, fancy dress, swinging boats etc. The highlight was the raffle on the last night. The prizes where always good. We won a dining room suite ourselves one year. We were delighted about that. At the time the church was repaired there was a Dominican Priest Fr Buckley who painted a beautiful fresco at the back of the alter depicting the crowning of Our Lady as Queen of Heaven. Even up to this day people who visit the church are drawn to this beautiful painting. Fr Mullin is gone but his memory lives on.

Mooncoin

In September 1955 I should have been leaving the Presentation School. But some of us were encouraged to stay on a year. It was a brilliant decision. We learned elocution, typing, short hand, and book keeping. Then in 1956 we had to decide where we were going. A good number of our class went to the Mercy Convent Waterford, but some including myself went to Mooncoin Vocational School. We were happy there from day one. We cycled the 6 miles to Mooncoin. There was about 6 girls and 5 or 6 boys from the boy's school in Kilmacow. We all travelled together. We were singing and laughing and having fun and never minded the journey. The teachers where Mr Doran (science) Mrs Laurigan (Maths and Commerce) Miss Kinnly (Domestic Science) Mr Connolly (Irish) and Mr Buckley (Woodwork). I liked the sense of having more freedom. It was only natural that we were encouraged to take a little more responsibility for our own actions. Mr Doran was one of life's gentlemen and he instilled in us a love and respect of the earth and animals. He encouraged also to treat everyone as equal. Mrs Laurigan taught us maths and commerce she was a lovely lady and we all liked her. Mr Connolly taught us Irish he was from West Cork and you couldn't have got a better person to teach Irish. I always liked Irish myself so I was happy enough. Miss Kinnly taught us Domestic Science. The poor girl would have had to perform a major miracle to teach me sewing as I had an Innate dislike to it and still do to this day. Another happy memory of Mooncoin was when we went to the Spring Show. It was always held in May I loved cycling to the main road where we joined the bus bound for the spring show. There was great excitement and banter. It usually happened to be a bright sunny day and we went round the grounds in groups happy to be with our friends and overwhelmed by all the different activities taking place. We always had a nice lunch and there was ample opportunity to get a small gift for Mam and Dad.

Photo in Mooncoin Vocational School in 1956, Maura back row 3rd in from left

One thing I noticed on the bus coming home there was a faint smell of cigarette smoke. I tried one myself once but it was the same size when we came home as it was when I left Dublin. So I never tried again but gave it up as a bad job. When we got home it was very dark, but dad met me at the bus and we cycled home together at the end of a perfect day.

At that time the group cert was the certificate recognised as having reached an acceptable level of education for our age. Ann Comerford of Kilnaspic got first place in Ireland one year for her Commerce exam. This merited that we all got a day off from school. When we returned after having the day off the girls were all saying they would love another day off. I said "don't worry girls I'll get a day off for you next year, I'll come first in sewing"! This brought a great laugh and Miss Kinnly wanted to know what we were laughing at. No one told her. But it ended up that I had to stay back for half an hour after school, and my friends from Kilmacow where looking in the window at me. We eventually got home none the worse of the ordeal.

Above Picture taken At Mooncoin Vocational School in 1956

A few years ago my husband Ollie and I paid a visit to Mount Mellary, Cappaquin. We happened to see this poem in the Souvenior Shop and Ollie took a great liking to it. I bought it for him on that day. I hope you all enjoy it as much as we have.

THE WORLD NEEDS

A little more kindness and a little less creed,

A little more giving and a little less greed;

A little more smile and a little less frown,

A little less kicking a man when he's down;

A little more "we" and a little less "I",

A little more laugh and a little less cry;

A few more flowers on the pathway of life,

And fewer on graves at the end of the strife.

Wild Life

A big loss to the little children today is that because of danger and evil so prevalent in the world today it is not safe to let children to school or anywhere on their own.

When we were going to school we had great fun in the evenings, playing hop scotch and other games. The boys played marbles. Nicholas and his friends used to go out with ferrets and terriers and it was customary for them to bring home a rabbit or two which Mam would prepare and cook the next day. The rabbit was also used in hospitals and was frequently served at dinner time. My xomatosis was spread through the rabbit population and it wasn't safe to eat them anymore.

We had a wonderful time when the mushrooms came into season. We used to go out at the break of day and look in the fields that had been pointed out to us. We went around the fields searching diligently until we had picked a big container of mushrooms. By this time we could see the smoke rise up from the chimney of the houses that were down from the fields. We brought the mushrooms home, Mam would put some of them on top of the old Stanley range which was red hot. They would be left to cook after which they were put on a dish, sprinkled with salt and there you have it a delicacy beyond compare. The best of the commercially grown ones couldn't hold a candle to them.

The Creamery

You could say the creamery together with the church, schools and post offices was the hub of the village. As the farmers lined up with their milk churns drawn by horse and cart or in the case of the small farmer by donkey and cart. I remember in Kilmacow creamery the dairymaid made the butter. They sold feeding stuff for animals. They also sold electrical goods and hard ware. The last creamery manager ran a very successful grocery shop which sold everything from a pin to an anchor. The social end of things came naturally as the farmers bought the daily papers. While waiting for their milk to be taken in, politics and local problems would be discussed and a lot of advice given. As the farmers made their way home after attending to their business in the creamery they had plenty to exercise their minds. Did they know what an asset the creamery was to the Kilmacow area. It was because of the creamery, the local shop did well as people came to buy papers and other commodities. If the creamery had not been open, their money would have been spent elsewhere. The same was the case concerning the post office. When the men prepared to go to the creamery, the women would sometimes go with them and visit the post office to post letters, pay bills and send parcels etc to friends and relatives living in other parts of the world.

My youngest daughter Olive was very fond of Kitty Flavin RIP. Kitty was extremely gifted with her hands and her craftwork was second to none. She held a craft evening every Monday night in her house. One evening she enquired from Olive if her Mammy would like to join them to do some crafts to which Olive replied "Mammy isn't able to sew" Kitty said "well teach her" to which Olive replied "you won't teach my Mammy, even the nuns gave up on her".

The Life of a Traveller

I also remember that those days were the days of the travelling people in Ireland. Families of them travelled in horse drawn caravans around Ireland. To me a child at that time it seems a very exciting life. What I didn't realise that they had to endure a lot of hardship, such as staying in wet clothes all day, overcrowding in the caravans, and maybe having to sleep under canvas. The women would go from house to house asking for tea, sugar or milk, or anything else they would be lucky enough to pick up. Mam always gave them what she could spare and she said that she was never at a loss because of it.

There was one family in particular who it seems had been calling since my Grandmothers time. She used to call every few months. Mam would make the tea and they would relax and have a chat. I played with her daughters and I would give them an old doll or teddy and some old copies of the Girls Crystal my favourite weekly at that time. Since those days my opinion of travellers has been there are some good, some bad the same is the case with the settled people. There is an old saying

"There is so much bad in the best of us.
And so much good in the worst of us.
That it ill beholds the best of us to speak about the rest of us".

Alot of the travellers were blessed with being able to perform certain D.I.Y jobs confidently. They excelled most of all at mending pots and pans. Thus it was that the farmers and country folk would bring all their damaged tin wear to the farmers work shop and the Tin Smith would make his way to the work shop. Soon he would set to work. When he was finished he would be delighted to see an array of gleaming tins before him.

One instant I will always remember is one morning it was quite dark. Mam, Paddy and myself were walking to Kilmacow train station on route to Dublin. When we were after travelling about a mile we came upon a most beautiful sight. There was a gap at the side of the road. Parked at the side was the travellers caravan but what really caught my attention was a huge fire. The flames were so bright and sitting round on stones and stools were a group of travellers singing and playing tin whistles. I know you may think that it could be different next morning but that early morning they created a scene of beauty that will stay with me always.

Christmas Customs

This story would not be complete without mentioning the Christmas customs in our area at that time. Once the Christmas devotions were over and everyone was happy. A few of our neighbours and ourselves got together and decided to make the week following Christmas a week of local music and crack. It worked liked this. There were about five families involved and we went to a different house each night. The house would be prepared that day. The room where the music took place would be nice and cheerful. After the first night we had a flavour of what was going to happen. Young and old alike came. Some brought musical instruments. The music started and the dancing got into full swing. During the night everyone did their party piece. There was a stop for tea and refreshments, which was given by the hostess. But everyone was anxious to get back to the dancing, singing and storytelling. It was a great night. We all went home happy and hungry for more.

The custom went on for a few years but it has died away over time, as a more affluent way of life has taken over. Whether it be for better or worse only time will tell.

Conclusion

It makes me happy to be able to say truthfully this year 2015 that I have witnessed a most wonderful dream which I have harboured in my heart for more years that I care to remember.

It became a reality for me today. That dream was to write a book and to have it published.

Since my school years I have enjoyed writing essays. My brother Paddy and I used to go to play with Mary my cousin regularly.

I never wanted to play much so I used to try and skip away and Aunt Alice would bring down children's books that Mary was sent every few months from America.

While I read those books it was if I was transported to another world. They were magic.

I would now like to thank all of you who have travelled with me on this journey. I hope you have enjoyed the experience as much as I have enjoyed sharing it with you and I look forward to all of you accompanying me on the next part of my journey of "A Walk Down Memory Lane". Which will be very soon please god.

Acknowledgements

I want to acknowledge the fact that I have stayed healthy and well both in mind and body to be inspired to write this book. Without our health we cannot achieve anything.

There are some people I have to thank, without whose help this book would not be completed.
First of all my husband Ollie, who is there to help me whatever the need and there are many but he is the one who is with me 24/7. He is my rock. Thank you Ollie.

To my daughters Annmarie & Olive, their husbands Sean & Shane, my 3 grandchildren Bethany, Aoibheann & Taylor who mean so much to me. They are very supportive & are my life.

To Mary & Vincent Predergast who are so helpful & are so willing to give their time to me. Thank you both.

To Choice Publishing who were so helpful to me whilst I was writing this book.

I would like to thank Con Doyle Photography, from Athy, Co. Kildare for the beautiful photograph on the back cover.

To Rory Williams (Country Style Foods) who sponsored me in this venture, and who with his Dad Sean, has sponsored me through the years in the many charities that Ollie has been involved in. Thanks Rory.

To The Irish Kidney Association, Waterford Branch who kindly agreed to combine our fundraising campaign to support my first publication of this book.

I would also like to thank Sean Mc Carthy for providing the photos of Tramore and Guchies Lane and also Joe Cashin for providing the photo for the front cover.

And last but not least thank you to all the readers for purchasing my book. I hope you enjoy reading it as much as I have done writing it. Hope you will continue to support me in the future.

Saint Senans Church, Kilmacow, Co. Kilkenny, where I was a sacristan for 18 years.

Some of you may be aware but some of you may not that I was a sacristan in our local church Saint Senan's, Kilmacow, for 18 years. One evening the priest as that time was rushing home ahead of me. I just happened to say the following words to him and this became his sermon the following Sunday.

Don't Walk Before Me I May Not Follow
Don't Walk Behind Me I May Not Lead
Just Walk Beside Me And Be My Friend.

Guchies Lane is a scenic walk between the Upper and Lower village of Kilmacow

~ 65 ~